BENEDICT NNOLIM: MODERN TIMES REVISITED

MODERN TIMES REVISITED

Benedict Nnolim

Published September 5, 2012

ISBN 978-1-906914-79-0

Other Books of Poetry by Ben Nnolim Books on www.lulu.com

Title	Paperback	Hardback	eBook
Mr Goodman and Other Poems	978-1-906914-14-1	978-1-906914-68-4	978-1-906914-32-5
Dialogue	978-1-906914-03-5	978-1-906914-57-8	978-1-906914-29-5
Graffiti	978-1-906914-07-3	978-1-906914-58-5	978-1-906914-31-8
They sold Us Mud	978-1-906914-53-0	978-1-906914-67-7	978-1-906914-50-9
Modern Times	978-1-906914-76-9		

Ben Nnolim Books
7 Sandway Path,
St. Mary Cray,
Orpington. Kent
BR5 3TS, UK
Email: benedictnnolim@aol.com

DEDICATION

This book is dedicated to
all people of good conscience

Preface

All civilizations have one thing in common: they rise, bestride their region of the world for a time, sometimes for centuries, and then die. This death occurs either by external conquest or by internal decadence but is never a quick process.

It seems that civilizations, and the people in them, never learn from history. Considering that the twentieth, to the twenty first, century is the only period, so far, in human history, in which the most is known about the world and about human existence, one would have expected this period to be one of near ideal, amicable and mature relationships among the peoples who make up the human race.

Instead, fantastic intellectual, technological and social developments and achievements, jostle, for pre-eminence, with brutal wars, individual selfishness, disregard of cohesive social conventions, and resurgence of ancient vices and customs (which led to the decline and fall of earlier civilizations).

It seems that whatever praiseworthy progress the human race makes, it wants to take back by acting as if it wants to go back to primitive times and start all over again.

Democracy, human rights, civil rights, freedom of choice and thought, of religion and of association, ideals long sought after, and fought for, over many centuries of tyranny and cruelty, seem near to achievement in modern times.

The enjoyment of these, however, seems to be hindered, and in some cases, prevented outright, by a hedonistic, intolerant but powerful minority who claim to subscribe to these ideals but, in reality, deny decent citizens their own democracy, human rights and freedoms.

Fortunately, in every civilization and culture and since ancient times, there have always been individuals, thinkers, singers, poets, politicians, comedians, etc, who make it their duty to observe and comment on the affairs of their day. They, either eulogize the achievements of the day, satirize them or, condemn them but in all cases, provide some sort of record, for coming generations, of their life and times.

The poems in this book represent one of many, such commentaries on modern times. They are kaleidoscopic in the sense that they address many, varying and different issues, the personal, the societal, the political, the moral, the religious, etc. They are tunnel visioned in the sense that their perspective is Christian, even if broadminded and non parochial.

The poems, in this book, may not be the types that giants such as Virgil, Dante, Shakespeare, Ovid, Dryden, Wordsworth, Keats, to name but a few, would write. They are, however, what may be called, at best, modern, popular poetry, in everyday international English so that the reader does not need an expert to explain their meaning.

The important thing, however, is that you, the reader, enjoy the experience.

Good reading.

Benedict Nnolim

September 5, 2012

TABLE OF CONTENTS

NICE PEOPLE

People are not nice.
Don't get me wrong; there are nice people.
There are, even, people who are very nice.
But these are few and far between.

Being nice is just a game,
which, it seems, you have to play,
if you want to get along;
easier too than being, really, nice.

All you have to do,
is to look, or appear to be, nice,
talk and act as if you're nice,
none of which is hard to do.

Even if you tell a lie,
tell it nicely and with charm.
Even if you ruin a name,
do it nicely and with style.

Woe betide you, in your days,
if you do not play the game,
or lose concentration in your game.
I dare not tell you of your fate.

If you ever tell a truth,
you will find, indeed, in truth,
how wicked, nasty, intolerant,
these nice and gentle people, really, are.

PREJUDICE

A bully's illness at its worst,
a family sickness where they're born.
So bad and shameful it's unheard,
it had to hide in camouflage.

If this camouflage will work,
a good scapegoat, a well known word,
must be found to take the rap;
what better word than prejudice?

Prejudice is prejudgement;
throughout our lives, it's what we do.
We think, we talk, we implement,
not before we judge its good.

What we see and what we do
must, from start, be pigeonholed.
If it isn't classified,
none believes it makes any sense.

At times we're right,
at times we're wrong;
without prejudging,
we're often lost.

My view, of it, you may dispute;
any step you take in life
must be done with prejudice,
if you do not want to die.

Prejudice, in life, is it.
We do not jump before we see.

If the facts, at last, don't fit,
in bad results, it's prejudice.

In all our lives, it does its part
in great discoveries and the arts.
It gives us classes, types and kinds
and helps decipher nature's kinds.

There is nothing wrong with thoughts
or prejudgement of our choice.
Life is nought without our thoughts
and, quite, unsafe without forethought

It helps us too, in strange surrounds,
to feel secure amid unknowns.
Whites and blacks and all the sins;
terrible illness blamed on it.

You hurt, you hang, discriminate,
those you think are not like you,
or are weak, unversed in sin,
in jest, for business or for trade.

4

You won't admit you're sick and ill.
You find a name for your evil deeds.
You call your illness, prejudice,
and seek a cure by fighting it.

It is unfair to prejudice
to blame these terrible sins on it.
It is a sickness at its peak,
camouflaged as prejudice.

Kid yourself as you would like,
but leave prejudgement out of it.
For what you are you won't admit;
you are sick not prejudiced.

PEASANT GIRL

They laughed at us, the joke was us,
peasant people, poor and weak,
in the towns of modern times.

Dad was poor and so was Mum,

but my brothers did not care.
There is life in alley ways,
in the towns of modern times.

But, for me, I took an oath,
a peasant girl I will not be.
Peasant girls are country girls,
not of towns in modern times.

To fight, I must, a way to find,
to stop this life of peasant girl.
I cannot be a peasant girl
in the towns of modern times.

So I set myself the task
to do the things we hear they do.
I went to school and did like them.
I did the plays and literature,
as they do in modern times.

I did the dates, like all of them,
pretty dresses, teasing men.

But peasant girls they do not tease;
they give and take it as it is,
much preferred in modern times.

Every chance I saw I took.
Getting into fruitful parts,
no convictions, play the part;
in modern times, it's what they do.

Now I've got their everything;
was it worth the task I ask?
I find I'm still a peasant girl.
Perhaps, it's genes or DNA,
or perhaps it's modern times.

I KNOW A FRIEND

I know a friend who loves his God
with a fervour that's unheard.
In all he does and all he says;
his God must be the first and last.

When they talk, I do not know;
where they meet, I cannot say.
But there's nothing that he does
without approval by his God.

It makes me wonder, every time,
whether his God is same as mine.
The God I know is power and love;
a kind and gentle, generous, God.

But my friend, in spite of being,
sworn, attached and bound to his God,
who rules and guides his every being,
seems to have a miserable lot.

It makes you think; it makes you see
why some think there can't be God.
How can there be any God
who cannot help my friend in need?

But my friend, he thinks they're blind.
So many miracles in his life

has left him, right and left, convinced
that his God is great and kind.

THE GODLY KIND

Of all the kinds, in modern times,
the most oppressed, the Godly kind.
It doesn't matter who their God
their main offence to have a God

To have a God is to bind yourself
to rules and life you may not like.
This is bad in modern times
where the rule is selfishness.

The Godly kind are not much fun.
Their lives are full of dos and don'ts.
This is sin and this is wrong.
How, on earth, can life be fun?

What is life if not of fun?
What is life without a pun?

9

How can one go through this life,
always careful and in strife?

But these, contend the Godly kind,
are the reasons for their life.
Life is good and lots of fun,
if all of us are part of God.

Think of it, a world of love,
and all desires are of God.
There's no greed; there's no lust.
In all you do you want to be just.

There's no fear of being betrayed.
There's no fear of cheats.
No one tells a lie or fibs.
Every deal is fair and square.

To add to these, and when you die,
you will go to Paradise,
whose greatest treat must, surely, be
face to face and there with God.

10

But the rest, the unGodly kind,
think that all of this is bunk.
That is why, in modern times,
life is hard for the Godly kind.

NINCOMPOOPS

It's so sad it makes you cry
It's so bad you wish you'd cracked.
How can things like this apply,
of all times, in modern times?

We know there's good, we know there's bad.
We know there're, even, ugly things.
But for evil straight from hell;
it isn't fair, we're not in hell.

Some are wise, they take advice.
Some are smart and know the stops.
But the fools and nincompoops;
they do not know and cannot stop.

Modern times must take the blame.
They claim they've made it from Stone Age,
where the mighty, savage, throng
have no time for right and wrong.

Nincompoops are so naive.
Tricked and conned, they're easy prey.
Trusting, faithful to a fault;
they, just, don't get it, what's in stock.

They do not know that all the hype
of good and bad of modern times,
of noble deeds and heroes' acts
are just fronts to get along.

They do not know and can't believe
that people hype but don't believe
all those good and noble deeds
which bring the doer only tears.

IF A FOOL AND NINCOMPOOP

If you're a fool and nincompoop,
in the eyes of modern times,
do not fret or think you're doomed,
but take your time to clear your mind.

In modern times, the nincompoops
are those guys who keep to rules,
who fret about unfaithful word
or failing friends in deed or thought.

Modern times has many rights
and wrongs and types of various kinds;
Christian rights, Muslim rights,
Buddhist, Hindu, Human Rights.

Christian rights are much maligned;
Muslim rights most nearly so.
Buddhist, Hindu, rights in mists;
Human Rights, for now, is king.

.

13

If this king you don't obey,
but stick to Christian, Muslim rights,
or to Buddhist, Hindu, rights,
Human Rights will hound and prey.

WHY DO YOU ASK?

I will tell you what I think
after I've got and had my drink.
One, two, three are parts of it;
five and six and that is it.

Why do you ask? What is it?
Don't you know or can't you think?
What is new in what I do,
what you do or what they do?

In all our lives, we look the same;
two eyes, two ears and legs and all.
Yet each has a different face,
and think and talk in different ways.

It makes you mad, it makes me sad;
why we're same but not the same.
Knowing things that we all like,
yet doing things I do not like.

Is it me to take the blame,
or you or they or anyone?
Truth is many, hard to take;
why not seek than fighting me?

ENJOY TODAY, TOMORROW DIE

Enjoy today, tomorrow die;
is a saying I have heard.
In every age, in every land
a tribe exists who think it fact.

If they're few we do not know.
If they're many, who will count?
But come the chance and you will see
who is who, who such believe.

Life is nature, nature life.
With no push or shove it's vain.
Yet it goes on at its pace;
not your pace or mine.

But human beings, they do not rest.
Knowing little, caring less,
they push and shove in mindless zest,
causing sorrow, loss and death.

If today you enjoy yourself
and, come tomorrow, you are dead.
What of those, tomorrow's dead
who miss today's enjoyment day?

MODERN TIMES

Modern times, that's where we are;
Albert Einstein, and his kind,
keep us baffled with their thoughts-
E is, certainly, mc squared.

Leptons, muons, bosons, gluons,
Higgs, a boson, of his own.
Up down quarks and bottom top quarks,
some are strange, some even charmed.

.

Energy is dark and matter dark;
and both, we're told, are well conserved.
Gravity waves, they baffle maths.
Our sun is just a ball of gas.

There is Darwin and his kind,
patient, careful, rigorous,
who do their best to make some sense
of our life and being on earth.

Alas, we are but human beings,
in or out of modern times.
There are, always, some of us,
who use his views in blasphemy.

We can't forget the medical men
who, for sure, do save more lives

17

than those of us who will be God,
who clone and stem cell, stifling birth.

Where on earth will all these be,
if ignored, the digital kids?
What appliance, what we do,
is not based on what they do?

What of governments of the world,
who cheat and lie to stay on top,
who make democracy a kind of god,
yet don't believe in it one jot.

There's the press, both, free or fair,
in papers, TV and the air.
They make a lot about free press,
but cause the problems of the times.

All the achievements of our times,
in spite of all that we have got,
it seems that we are in a pot,
overheating, about to burst.

Our past achievements, we agree,
were built on blood and wickedness.
Our pot has burst in recent times,
in the first and second Wars.

It looks like time is ripe again
for the boiling pot to burst.
Wars and bombings everywhere,
safety valves not quite enough.

Things are hard in modern times.
No surprise that this is so.
Faith in God has lost its shine.
There is no anchor to our lives,

SOCIALISM AND THE REST

I can see the reason now
why there's angst in every place.
Some are rich and some are poor;
but that's not why there's so much angst.

They say they're civilised.
They say they're fair to all.
But look around in all they do
and see the people in the moon.

The Greeks were civilised;
it turns out helots were not so.
Romans, too, were civilised;
countless slaves, they thought not so.

Egypt, Persia, kingdoms then;
all of them were civilised.
The only people just nowhere
were my people, Africans.

My! It's great to civilise,
living cheek by jowl all day.
You learn your manners, tolerance,
and how delightful are the arts.

You can kill and go to war
and rob and pillage in the act.

As long as you have won the war
you are very civilised.

Take it down to modern times
to Europe, US and their kinds.
There, they call it civil rights,
voting rights and human rights.

If these are true, it must be right
to live in joy without a fear.
Those in this deceit believe
are just living in the clouds.

Truth is fact and fact is clear;
we are living in their cells.
These cells are prisons without walls;
but more secure than those with walls.

There's a lot of noise they make;
freedom, rights, in all their shades.
But what we really have and face
is a wicked total state.

21

There's no right, there's no wrong.
There's no slack in deed or thought.
What is right or what is wrong
is the economy and it's jobs.

So the poor in their despair
clutch at straws to save themselves.
The straw they catch is straight and weak;
hate and envy for the rich.

So they spend their lives in vain
seeking wealth or fighting it.
Socialism and all the rest
claim to be tools for the useless fight.

Oh my poor, my, Africa,
you knew it all before their time.
To live with nature and its mores
is the wisest act of time.

There is blemish in everything.
There's a wart on every face.

The logs before their eyes in spite;
they made a lot about your specks.

Fret not now about your state.
Do not moan about the past.
Note, beware, their wickedness.
Disregard their arrogance.

There's no hope for a peaceful man
among a people drunk with wars.
His only hope and comfort yet
will come in time when time will tell.

THEY USED TO HAVE A GOD

They used to have a God;
the one and, only, truly, God.
This God, He made the heavens and the earth
and everything within and without.

He was almighty, all knowing
and all loving.

His sun shone, His rains fell,
equally,
on the good and bad.

All those other gods of old,
from ancient Greece and Rome,
not to talk of Africa, the Pacific,
and the Far and the Middle East,
were merely idols
and proof
that this God was the true and only one.

What was it
that couldn't be done
in His name?
Genocides, wars, burnings at the stake;
anything
to establish His everlasting rule.

But truth, the real truth,
could it be coming out, at last?
Was this God an excuse

for doing things they had to do,
camouflaged in pious acts?

This God, this poor God;
is His time is up?
Is it time for newer gods?

Democracy, freedom, human rights;
animal rights, environment and more,
are these the new and wonderful gods?
Which of them will come out tops
and be the new God?

DEMOCRACY

Democracy, what, on earth, is it?
Democracy, who, on earth, believes in it?
They say some people do.

Governments, ancient and modern,
north, south, east and west, everywhere,
none, I've found, believes in it.

Priviledged, ancient, thoughtful, Greeks,
who denied helots their rights or votes;
get the credit for inventing it.

Europeans, governments and their elite,
who didn't think women or the landless fit
to vote,
are champions of democracy.

European dissidents, convicts, etc,
forced, desperate or willing immigrants
to the Americas,
who killed off the local inhabitants,
are champions of democracy.

Americans, north or south,
who didn't think the natives,
or their African slaves,
fit to vote,
are champions of democracy.

Poor democracy, championed by all;

26

Poor democracy, unchanged,
apparently, unchangeable in every age,
used by those in power,
with tinkering here and there,
to do whatever they like to do.

There used to be elections;
there used to be votes;
in a democracy.
At least, that is what we were told.

Rigged elections, falsified votes,
citizens not allowed to vote,
or excluded for one reason or the other,
put democracy in a parlous state.

The majority used to have its way,
the minority its say,
in a democracy.
But now it's the noisiest, not the right,
who have both their way and say.

If there is democracy, the kind they push,
why can't the Irish vote, instead of fight,
to be one or two?

If there is democracy, the kind they push,
why can't the Kurds vote, instead of fight,
to be in or out of Iran, Iraq or Turkey?

If there is democracy, the kind they push,
why is there fighting, and not votes,
in Iraq, in Afghanistan and now Syria,
not to talk of Libya?

If there is democracy, the kind they push,
why can't many more, than I can mention here,
vote
to be whatever they want to be?

If there is democracy, the kind they push,
why can't gays, lesbians and straights vote
to have their separate ways in law;
than have the taxes paid by each

fund the other's ways and different lives?

If there is democracy, the kind they push,
why can't the racists, bigots, nudists, and all vote
to live their lives as they would choose,
as long as each will not be kept,
or fed, by those not of their kind.

.

If there is democracy, the kind they push,
why are taxes and tax rates different
for different people and companies,
democratically,
citizens of the place?

If there is democracy, the kind they push,
why aren't we all agreed
on one personal allowance,
for all income tax,
one corporate allowance,
for all company tax?

If there is democracy, the kind they push,

why aren't we all agreed
on one tax rate,
the same exceptions, the same incentives,
for all personal income tax?

If there is democracy, the kind they push,
why aren't we all agreed
on one tax rate,
the same exceptions, the same incentives,
for all company tax?

No, it is not democracy yet;
at least, not the one they push.
At best, we may or may not be
on its learning curve,
and then, on its lowest point.

If and when we find we are,
shall we agree
to move up on its learning curve?
If we find we are not,
shall we agree

to adopt true democracy
or dump the idea altogether?

FREE PRESS

A lot is made of it.
A lot is said of it.
If you ask me what I think,
I'd say the free press is a joke.

It is claimed by everyone,
in loud propaganda by the West.
Official logic by the East,
makes its claim with heavy fiat.

In every case, the press is free
as long as power, money, race,
and their various arrangements
keep the circus on.

Who has ever gagged a press
that does its best to trumpet him?

What has ever gagged a press
that does its job of touting it?

Take a look at the freest press;
take a look at what they press.
Come with me and take a look
at things they shout at most.

If there are riots in their land,
it's the hooligans and their kind.
These are kettled, water cannoned,
mass arrested and in court.

The rave is, Prosecute!
by the free press quite outraged.
It howls in rage, it howls in anger,
for the government to inquire.

There's no rioter interviewed
on TV, anywhere.
What point of view can criminals have,
not better heard in court?

But let occur an altercation,
by groups, unknown, unsung,
in countries not allied with them,
a hue and cry is raised.

Oh, the long, suppressed, opposed,
robbed of freedom, and their rights,
struggling, fighting, dying so,
they need our help for human rights.

Every straggler interviewed,
coaxed, cajoled, to make a speech
that is suited to their game.
Breaking news, front headlines,
make these rascals instant stars.

Woe betide these terrible lands
if a riot, on the scale,
blamed on hooligans in their land,
occurs in countries not allied.

A revolution dawns, in sight,

33

and all their business stops.
A kind of spring has come to pass
and the chance must not be lost.

Military threats, all kinds of threats,
are pumped and fuelled by all the press.
Their saintly governments, why can't they
rush and save their friends oppressed?

Their saintly governments, why can't they,
by the treaties of the past,
parachute, install, by force,
democracy for their friends?

No one talks of votes, elections,
or of what majority thinks.
These, of course, can have no views
because the free press knows it best.

A war is urged to install, in haste,
democracy of the press;
not one voice is heard about

34

democracy of the people.

A war is urged to install, in haste,
democracy by the press;
not one voice is heard about
democracy by the people.

A war is urged to install, in haste,
democracy for the press;
not one voice is heard about
democracy for the people.

What will not the free press do
to get the tyrants in their sights?
All the tyrants that we know,
when we think we've got them licked,
rise, like phoenix, in new lives.

When we throw out kings and queens,
we find oligarchs in their place.
When we throw out oligarchs,
we find the free press in their place.

They say they're free but in cahoots
with the governments in their turf,
whose tyranny, oppression, repression,
they hardly talk about.

Allies of their governments,
and those that suit their trade,
no matter what their sins may be,
hardly make the news.

Struggling countries not allied,
harmless, powerless, on their own,
trying hard to get some peace,
amidst the tricks, intrigues, against,
are tarred and marred by the freest press.

The press, I'm sure, was free and fair
in South Apartheid Africa?
The press is totally good and free
in north and south America.

The world, you have to take my word,

will, surely, come to an end.
It will be sooner than you think,
when creating, as is now in us,
fizzles out and dies

The world, believe it if you like,
will, surely, come to an end.
It will be sooner than you think,
when right and wrong will look alike
and have the same respect.

The world will, certainly, come to an end
when one God is, finally, lost.
It won't be soon, I don't know when.
But come the time and all will have
a god for each and everyone.

Who works in manic and restless haste?
Who, loud and shrill, will drown all sense?
Who loves sensation more than sense?
Who wants, in haste, the world to end?
Could it be the modern press?

Strange it is, isn't it
that only when they're gagged,
that is when the modern press
will want the truth to be told?

Strange, and stranger still it is
that the press which wants the truth
is that one which is not free?

YOUR THOUSAND YEARS ARE HERE

Enjoy yourself.
Indulge yourself.
Your thousand years are here.

Feminise, equalise.
Empower all.
Your thousand years are here.

Contracept.
Abort and stem.
Your thousand years are here.

Homophile.

Paedophile.

Your thousand years are here.

Die by choice.

Kill by choice.

Your thousand years are here.

Grab your rights.

Only you have rights.

Your thousand years are here.

Previous rights,

now, current wrongs;

your thousand years are here.

Single mums;

fatherless homes;

your thousand years are here.

Divorcees;

cheating spouses;

your thousand years are here.

Bombs and shootings;
street massacres;
your thousand years are here.

God is myth,
His morals bunk;
your thousand years are here

All the Faiths
are myths and tales;
your thousand years are here.

Christophobe.
Islamophobe.
Your thousand years are here.

Evolution,
all is chance;
your thousand years are here.

Satan, demons,

count the years;

your thousand years will soon be up.

And when they're up,

your time is up.

Woes betide you and your gang.

WHO BELIEVES?

Who believes, who deceived,

who is, really, taken in

by this modern con?

Who promotes this; what is gained

from this endless search for endless ends?

This endless search for happiness;

a happiness that doesn't end.

Isn't it clear to one and all;

the brazen swagger, confidence,

assertiveness, and this demand

for this and that, all kind of rights,
are just cries and pleas for help?

The antiperspirants, the colognes,
the anti, wrinkle, aging creams,
the expensive rags they take as clothes,
not to talk of cleavage here and there,
are all cries and pleas for help.

What they truly want and crave
is just to be heard and understood;
to be noticed and truly loved,
and be taken as they are.

But you cannot run and chase as hares.
What is good or bad is well known.
Who will swear he doesn't know
what is true, what is just, what is fair?

Are these mere statistics or only fit to use
when they're breached against us?
Why is everyone's actions so contrary;

that all must be on guard?

Husbands, wives, they are afraid,
brothers, sisters, cousins, too.
Parents, children, they are afraid
and all of it in modern times.

Here they are, all grins and smiles,
and everything is very nice.
But take their pulse and look inside,
they are hurting, about to burst.

Who believes, who deceived,
who is, really, taken in
by this modern con?

This endless search for economic growth,
exports, always, on the rise,
head on collision course with normal life,
which has no such laws for growth.

Perpetual happiness,

perpetual economic growth;
exports always rising, only grow
at someone's expense.

It is known by one and all;
that nature has, and sets, limits,
that nature gives as well as takes,
to keep the earth alive and sane.

Who will tell them, when they know
everything that can be known?
Who will force them, when they are
strong and mightier than the rest?

Who will you, alas, believe,
when the Faiths are just, but, myths,
ancient fears and superstitions,
out of date in modern times?

Who will you believe and trust?
Who will show his softer side,
and not be seen as weak and ripe

to be bullied till he dies?

Are these not the ways of man?
Are these not the fruits of war,
of years of conflict and dissent,
in spite of progress on all fronts?

PSSSST!

Psssst!
Please, don't say I told you.
Please, don't mention my name or place
or I will be put in jail
for saying my mind
and what I think.

Don't ask me.
Don't even try,
or you, too, may be an accomplice
and, like me, be put in jail.

There are rights everywhere.

We are free to live our lives,
it is our human right.
But don't you say I told you so;
it's not for everyone,
unless you are gay, an atheist,
anti Christ and a humanist.

NOTHINK, NOSPEAK

Hey you! George, you great Orwell!
Hey you! George, remember these?
1984, Animal Farm,
and many other of your marvellous works;
how insightful, how predictive,
prophetic, of evolving time!

I'm sorry it has to be me,
and others too, maybe, perhaps,
who have to break the news to you
of sad and terrible things.

.

Newthink, Newspeak, and other speaks,

smart and clever in your days,
have now been well and truly shot
by Nothink, Nospeak and Nosense,
specialties of favourite talk and TV shows.

In your dreams, a ruling class,
a scheming, plotting, small cabal,
rising through the mob and ranks,
who served their ends in public good,
was the subject of your ire.

In modern times, we cannot say
who is who that rules the world,
as the rich, the noble, the destitute,
are, with scoundrels, in the gang.

Your Newspeak, Newthink, quite profound,
are much too much for this crowd.
Be Celeb or talked about,
whether for good or for ill,
none of which has any clout,
are the things that pay the bill.

What best can serve this modern mob
than Nothink, Nospeak and Nosense?
What can good sense, logic do
in these new and modern times?

THE CATHOLIC CHURCH

There are citizens everywhere
in every country of the world.
Some are thieves, some are rogues,
most are decent, lawful folks.

Every country has its laws
culture, mores and more.
The good, the lawful, in high regard;
the crooks are punished when they're caught.

Every country has its clubs,
and groups and places of their kinds.
Every club and place has its rules
for its members to behave.

Football clubs, cricket clubs,
all tennis and boxing clubs;
nobody tells them who will play
or the rules with which they play

In every club, its rules enforced,
in internal processes.
PhDs, and most degrees
are not given by the press.

All of these I must admit
are for the world and life on earth.
There is no talk of afterlife
except for your kith and kin.

Pity then the Catholic Church,
whose membership is a group of three,
with one group down here on earth,
the other two in afterlife.

The good, industrious, get rewards,
not in life but when they die.

The lawless, punished, out of sight,
not in life but when they die.

With these constraints, it's quite a job
to get its members, here, to behave.
Its faith is all in Jesus Christ
by whom assured it won't be lost.

Its rules are hard but not beyond
its serious members reach.
But those its rules who often breach
would run as hares and chase as hounds.

To be a Catholic is their aim
while the rules they will not keep.
They want to change the Catholic Church
to suit their aims, within their reach.

Their kinds are found in every place,
much like germs in cleaned up space.
They ruin, infest, and bring to rot,
everything they come to touch.

Once they bring the Church to rot,
you would think they're good and done.
No. They move to another club,
to ruin, infest, and bring to rot.

Take a guess at who they use
to publicise misguided views.
It is the press both free and fair
to sell the papers, adverts, fare.

The press would like the Catholic Church
to sing and dance its tune;
to install the priests and Popes it likes
and make its rules of right and wrong.

What is Church, if not a crowd,
that has to live and move with times?
What is God if not a myth,
that cannot block the profit lines?

INDEX OF FIRST LINES